Biblical Theology

Biblical Theology
A Proposal

Brevard S. Childs

Fortress Press
Minneapolis

BIBLICAL THEOLOGY
A PROPOSAL

Facets edition 2002

Adapted from *Biblical Theology of the Old and New Testaments: Theological Reflections on the Christian Bible*, copyright © Brevard S. Childs, 1992; Fortress Press edition 1993.

Cover and book design: Joseph Bonyata
Cover graphic: copyright © nonstøck inc. Used by permission.

0-8006-3481-0

The paper used in this publication meets the minimum requirements of American National Standard for Information Sciences—Permanence of Paper for Printed Library Materials, ANSI Z329.48-1984.

Manufactured in the U.S.A.   AF 1-3481

Contents

1
The History of Biblical Theology as a Discipline

The Development of the Discipline

It has long been recognized that the term "Biblical Theology" is ambiguous. It can either denote a theology contained within the Bible or a theology that accords with the Bible (Ebeling 1963:79). The first definition understands the task of Biblical Theology to be a descriptive, historical one that seeks to determine what was the theology of the biblical authors themselves. The second understands the task of Biblical Theology to be a constructive, theological one that attempts to formulate a modern theology compatible in some sense with the Bible. From one perspective, the entire modern history of the discipline of Biblical Theology can be interpreted as the effort to distinguish between these two definitions and to explore the important implications of the distinction.

The history of the discipline began to be first outlined in the nineteenth century in

monographs and in essays (Diestel 1869; Kähler 1896; Holtzmann 1911). Within the last few
decades, however, several detailed and highly
informative studies have broken fresh ground
in tracing the rise of this modern biblical discipline (see Kraus 1970; Merk 1972; Zimmerli
1980; Frei 1973; Stuhlmacher 1979; Gunneweg
1978). In addition, important books and articles
have pursued the individual contributions of
key figures (for example, Hornig on Semler;
Smend on de Wette and Gabler; Morgan on
Wrede and Schlatter). Finally, several comprehensive bibliographies of the modern debate
over Biblical Theology have recently appeared
which serve as valuable guides into the present
status of the discussion (for example, Reventlow 1986; Janowski 1986). For these reasons it
does not seem necessary once again to review
in detail this history of scholarship, but rather
to summarize the consensus and to focus on the
hermeneutical and theological implications
which derive from the history.

There is general agreement that Biblical Theology as a discrete discipline within the field of
biblical studies is a post-Reformation development. Although the Bible was much studied
earlier, it is argued that during the period of the
early and medieval church the Bible functioned
within a dogmatic ecclesiastical framework in a
subservient role in order to support various traditional theological systems. The Reformation
signaled a change in emphasis by its appeal to

the Bible as the sole authority in matters of faith, nevertheless the Reformers provided only the necessary context for the subsequent developments without themselves making the decisive move toward complete independence from ecclesial tradition. Only in the post-Reformation period did the true beginning of a new approach emerge.

Kraus has made the interesting case that already at the end of the sixteenth century there had appeared a form of "dogmatic biblicism" (e.g., Flacius 1580), but the actual term "Biblical Theology" was first used in the seventeenth century (Kraus 1970:18ff.; see the debate in Ebeling 1963; Merk 1972). The adjectival use of the term biblical, which at first seems tautological when defining Christian theology, derives from the polemical context out of which a new understanding of the Bible emerged. On the one hand, German pietists objected to the dominance of scholasticism and they appealed rather to a theology based solely on the Bible, that is, to a Biblical Theology. On the other hand, rationalists called for a return to the "simple" and "historical" religion of the Bible apart from the complex ecclesiastical formulations, that is, to a Biblical Theology. It is hardly surprising therefore that, in a four-volume *Biblische Theologie* (1771–72), G. T. Zachariä fused the elements of pietism with rationalism, and struggled for a historical interpretation while still assuming the church's doctrine of scriptural inspiration.

The widely recognized significance of Johann Philipp Gabler lies in his attempt to establish methodological clarity respecting the subject matter of Biblical Theology. In his now famous lecture of 1787 he set out in the title his basic concern: "A discourse on the proper distinction between biblical and dogmatic theology and the correct delimination of their boundaries" (see the ET 1980). Gabler began by sharply distinguishing Biblical Theology that he characterized as a historical discipline from dogmatic theology that he described as didactic in nature. He argued that much of the confusion regarding the Bible had arisen by mixing religion that was transparent and simple with theology that was subtle, subjective and changeable. Gabler then proceeded to set forth various exegetical steps for properly handling the Bible as a historical discipline.

First, the text was to be carefully studied and classified according to its historical period, authorship, and linguistic convention. A second step involved a comparison of the various parts in order to discern the agreement or disagreement of the different biblical authors much as one would handle any other system of philosophy. Only when the interpreter had filtered the biblical material through these two stages was he prepared for the crucial third step of distinguishing in the material that which was universally true from the temporal. This "pure Biblical theology" was then in a form suitable for reflection by dogmatic theology. It was fully consistent with Gabler's hermeneutics when he subsequently made specific the distinction between *auslegen* (which was a philological historical interpretation of the text) and *erklären* (which was an attempt to determine the true causes lying behind the particular construals).

In spite of the clarity of Gabler's appeal for a historical reading of the Bible, other factors shortly entered that blurred the developments of the discipline. Seen from Gabler's perspective, the next generation of scholars such as Ammon and de Wette confused his historical criterion by introducing a heavily philosophical reading under the influence of Kant and de Fries, which again focused on symbolic interpretation of ethical concepts from the Bible. The first serious application of Gabler's hermeneutical system emerged in the two-volume Biblical Theology of Georg Lorenz Bauer, who for the first time separated the discipline into an Old Testament and a New Testament theology. The significance of this move not only reflected the growing complexity of the discipline, but far more importantly the growing conviction that the historical discontinuities between the testaments defied all attempts to maintain a traditional canonical unity.

The history of Biblical Theology throughout the nineteenth century and well into the early twentieth century shows clearly the effect of the emancipation of the discipline from its dependency on ecclesiastical doctrine. First of all, with few exceptions the field divided into two separate disciplines of Old and New Testament theologies, which at first continued to retain the term Biblical Theology. Even Martin Kähler conceded that this division was inevitable. In his article on Biblical Theology in the *TRE*, Walther Zimmerli (1980) pursued the history of Old Testament and Biblical Theology by tracing a line from Bauer, Vatke, Ewald, Oehler, and Schultz into the twentieth century. Otto Merk, in his companion article (1980), followed a New Testament trajectory from Baur, Hofmann, Weiss, Holtzmann, Kähler, and Wrede into the twentieth century. Significantly, Gabler's legacy of an historical approach as constitutive of Biblical Theology was almost universally assumed by both conservative (Oehler, Weiss) and liberal scholars (Schultz, Holtzmann).

Secondly, along with the concern to maintain the independence of Biblical Theology from dogmatic theology, there went a search for a new philosophical framework by which to integrate the biblical material over and above a straightforward historical reading. Various forms of philosophical idealism dominated the early nineteenth century, such as the Hegelianism of Baur and Vatke. Even the quite fresh construals of von Hofmann and Ewald reflected a heavy mixture of romantic and idealistic tendencies that often continued to be filtered through systematic theologies such as Schleier-macher's. By the end of the nineteenth century the impact of various concepts of historical evolution became pervasive (see Schultz) and were joined with the earlier philosophical theories of the growth of humanity through organic stages (C. F. Heyne). Ironically, even those scholars who strove for a more objective description of the diversity within the Bible, often fell back into portraying different doctrinal systems (Weiss) that satisfied neither the demands of historical nor theological coherence.

Thirdly, among many critical scholars there was a growing assumption that Biblical Theology as an academic discipline was largely anachronistic and was an unfortunate vestige from a past era. Gunkel expressed this general attitude toward Biblical Theology in a classic essay when he summarized all the history-of-religion's arguments against Biblical Theology and concluded:

> The recently experienced phenomenon of Biblical Theology's being replaced by the history of Israelite religion is to be explained from the fact that the spirit of historical investigation has now taken the place of a traditional doctrine of inspiration (1927:1090–91).

At least for a time that extended well into the twentieth century, it looked as if Gunkel's characterization was being confirmed.

Ebeling's Suggestions
for Redefining the Discipline

By the end of the nineteenth century the full
problematic of Biblical Theology had emerged
with great clarity. On the one hand, Gabler's
case for the independence of Biblical Theology
from dogmatic constraints appeared to many to
be fully justified. On the other hand, the pursuit
of Biblical Theology as a historical discipline
had resulted in the dissolution of the very discipline itself. In the light of this situation, it was
a major contribution of Gerhard Ebeling in the
1950s to have clarified the full dimensions of
the problems that confronted Biblical Theology
in the wake of the historical study of the Bible
by means of a classic essay (ET 1963).

Ebeling makes the following points. First, the
theological unity of the Old and New Testaments has become extremely fragile, and it
seems now impossible to combine the testaments on the same level in order to produce a
unified theology. Secondly, the inner unity of
each of the respective testaments has been cast
into such doubt that a theology of the New Testament consists largely in classifying the discrete theologies of its different authors. Thirdly,
the study of the Old and New Testaments as a
historical discipline can no longer be limited to
the so-called canonical scriptures since this
category is ultimately dogmatic and ecclesiastical. Rather, the use of all historical sources that

are pertinent to the subject is required without distinction. Finally, the strongest objection has arisen even to the application of the term "theology" in describing the contents of the Bible. At least the term "religion" should be substituted and the traditional terminology of revelation eschewed within the historical enterprise.

In sum, the basic question which has emerged in the aftermath of Gabler's defining of the enterprise as a historical discipline is to what extent the subject matter has been so dismantled as to call into question its very existence and viability. Before this challenge Ebeling has then attempted to address the problem in a programmatic fashion by redefining the discipline of Biblical Theology. He writes:

> Its task would accordingly be defined thus: In "biblical theology" the theologian who devotes himself specially to studying the connection between the Old and New Testaments has to give an account of his understanding of the Bible as a whole, i.e., above all of the theological problems that come of inquiring into the inner unity of the manifold testimony of the Bible. (1963:96)

Ebeling's redefining of the task of Biblical Theology has, in my opinion, made a valuable start toward reconstituting the field. However, because Ebeling has not in fact pursued his proposal further since its publication in 1955 (ET 1963), I would like to explore his proposal according to my own concept of the field. I am aware that Ebeling would have developed this definition in a different fashion, but I am grateful for his stimulus and initial insight.

First, Ebeling's definition is, in one sense, a return to a pre-Gabler position in so far as he once again joins the historical and theological elements. The task of Biblical Theology is defined as a modern theologian's reflection on various aspects of the Bible. The task is not confined simply to a historical description of the original author's intention. It is not surprising that recently others who have sought to reconstitute Biblical Theology, have also attacked the Gabler legacy of a sharp separation between the historical and the theological components (see Kraus 1970; Breukelman 1980:9–20; Ollenburger 1985). When Krister Stendahl defended once again (1965) his earlier position of the sharp distinction between the historical and the theological aspects of Biblical Theology (1962), his respondent, Avery Dulles, expressed his deep methodological misgivings. "Theology in its completeness is an undivided whole, in which biblical and systematic elements are inextricably intertwined" (Dulles 1965:216). Obviously, just how the two elements relate must be further debated, but the need for the two aspects to interact from the start seems basic for any new Biblical Theology.

Secondly, there is an important aspect in which Gabler's original proposal has been fully sustained by Ebeling. The task of Biblical Theology does not contain an essential, descriptive component in which Old and New Testament specialists continue to make clear "the manifold testimony of the Bible." Any new approach to the discipline must extend and indeed develop the Enlightenment's discovery that the task of the responsible exegete is to hear each testament's own voice, and both to recognize and pursue the nature of the Bible's diversity. However, an important post-Enlightenment correction is needed which rejects the widespread historicist's assumption that this historical goal is only objectively realized when the interpreter distances himself from all theology.

Thirdly, the biblical theologian's reflection is directed to the connection between the Old and New Testaments in an effort "to give an account of his understanding of the Bible as a whole . . . inquiring into its inner unity." Biblical Theology has as its proper context the canonical scriptures of the Christian church, not because only this literature influenced its history, but because of the peculiar reception of this corpus by a community of faith and practice. The Christian church responded to this literature as the authoritative word of God, and it remains existentially committed to an inquiry into its inner unity because of its confession of the one gospel of Jesus Christ that it proclaims to the world. It was therefore a fatal methodological mistake when the nature of the Bible was described solely in categories of the history of religion, a move that could only develop in the direction of contesting the integrity of the canon and of denying the legitimacy of its content as theology.

Finally, it is highly significant that Ebeling still speaks of the "testimony" of the Bible. The implications of describing the subject matter of the Bible as witness are crucial in any redefining of the discipline. The role of the Bible is not being understood simply as a cultural expression of ancient peoples, but as a testimony pointing beyond itself to a divine reality to which it bears witness. To speak of the Bible now as scripture further extends this insight because it implies its continuing role for the church as a vehicle of God's will. Such an approach to the Bible is obviously confessional. Yet the Enlightenment's alternative proposal that was to confine the Bible solely to the arena of human experience is just as much a philosophical commitment. In sum, the paradox of much of Biblical Theology was its attempt to pursue a theological discipline within a framework of Enlightenment's assumptions that necessarily resulted in its frustration and dissolution.

As part of our reflection on the history of the discipline, it seems appropriate to evaluate the strengths and weaknesses of the current models for doing Biblical Theology. Only after this task has been done will there be an appeal made to earlier classic theological models as a means of enriching any new attempt of reconstituting the field of Biblical Theology.

2

The Problem of
the Christian Bible

Biblical Theology is by definition theological
reflection on both the Old and New Testament. It
assumes that the Christian Bible consists of a
theological unity formed by the canonical union
of the two testaments. But what is exactly meant
by "the Christian Bible"? What is the relation of
the whole to its parts? A highly complex series
of historical and theological problems are
involved even in defining the subject.

At the heart of the problem lie certain theological claims of the church regarding the Jewish scriptures. When the New Testament spoke
of the sacred writings (*hē graphē*), it had reference to the Jewish scriptures, which it simply
assumed to be authoritative for Christians. In
diverse ways the New Testament writers sought
to spell out the exact relation between these
sacred writings and their testimony concerning
Jesus Christ. Luke described Jesus himself interpreting from scripture "the things concerning
himself" (Luke 24:27). Paul spoke of scripture
"being written down for our instruction"

(1 Corinthians 9:10; 10:11), and the writer of the Pastorals assured his Christian readers that "all scripture is inspired by God and is profitable for teaching, for reproof, for correction, and for training in righteousness" (2 Timothy 3:16). However, when one asks what was the scope and precise form of the scripture that was taken over, and how was the appropriation made, then a host of complex historical questions arises.

The Form of the Jewish Scriptures at the Rise of Christianity

The study of this historical problem has gone through several clearly distinguishable phases. The church Fathers accepted uncritically the Jewish legend that, when the scriptures were burned after the fall of Jerusalem, God dictated the entire Jewish canon to Ezra (4 Ezra 14:37-48; see Ryle 1892:242ff.) Later in the sixteenth century Ezra's role in the closing of the canon was modified by Elias Levita to include the work of the men of the Great Synagogue, who after establishing the Hebrew Bible divided it into three parts. However, with the rise of historical criticism, especially during the nineteenth century, an attempt was made critically to establish the actual historical process by which the Hebrew canon took shape.

By the end of the century a widespread consensus had emerged, set forth in the handbooks of Wildeboer (1895), Buhl (1892), and Ryle

(1892), which envisioned three historical stages
to the process. The Pentateuch or Torah received
a closed canonical status in the latter half of the
fifth century, the date being confirmed by the
Samaritan schism. The canonization of the
prophetic corpus was next set before the close of
the third century and supported by the exclusion
of the book of Daniel about 165 B.C.E.The final
section, the so-called Writings, was thought to
be formed into a closed canonical collection
only at the end of the first century C.E.when at the
Synod of Jamnia (90 C.E.), the rabbis established
the official limits of the Jewish canon (see Eissfeldt's slight modification of this nineteenth-
century consensus, 1965:164ff.).

Since the end of World War II, there has been
a new and vigorous attempt to reassess the historical problem of the formation of the Hebrew
canon, stimulated in part by the discoveries
of Qumran. The result of this new enterprise
has been to call into question the nineteenth-
century historical consensus and to undercut
seriously some of the evidence on which the
reconstruction rested. For example, the Samaritan schism is now seen to be a lengthy process
that cannot easily be used to establish a fixed
terminus (see Purvis 1968; Coggins 1975). The
script and textual tradition of the Samaritan
Pentateuch place it in the Hasmonean period
rather than in the fourth century. Again, the
hypothesis of an Alexandrian canon by which to
interpret the narrower and larger canon of the

Jewish synagogue has been effectively destroyed by Sundberg. Finally, the decisive role of the "synod" of Jamnia in closing the third part of the Hebrew canon has been seriously undermined (see Lewis 1964; Leiman 1976). These discussions were at best scholastic debates that lacked the great significance attributed to them by Christian interpreters.

Equally important are the deep misgivings that have arisen about the model of three successive historical stages through which the formation of the Jewish canon developed. Recent scholarship has been made painfully aware of the lack of solid historical evidence by which to determine large areas of development. Theodore N. Swanson has mounted an interesting case that the third section of the Hebrew canon, the Writings, may have been a secondary canonical subdivision which was effected long after the scope of the non-Mosaic books had been fixed within the comprehensive category of the "Prophets." There is much evidence that the books assigned to the Writings continued in much flux for a long period (see Josephus). Then again, Clements has argued that there is no warrant for assuming that one canonical collection was firmly fixed before another began (1975:55). Rather, the two parts of the Law and the Prophets were joined within a flexible collection and both experienced expansion. Finally, Beckwith (1985:165) has picked up an earlier proposal of Margolis (1922:54ff.) that the three sections of the canon are not historical accidents, but "works of art." This is to say, that literary and theological factors were involved in the distribution and arrangements of the canon, and that the exclusion of Daniel from the Prophets, for example, may have been made from a theological and not historical judgment.

In sum, the crux of the problem is how to correlate elements of diversity with those of stability within the history of the growth of the Jewish canon without falling prey to the danger of extrapolating beyond the evidence in order to fill in the many gaps in our knowledge.

The Sources for Determining its Scope

We begin with the historical evidence regarding the form and scope of the Hebrew canon during the era shortly before and after the rise of Christianity. The Book of Sirach (Ben Sira or Ecclesiasticus) is dated about 180 B.C.E. and is an important testimony as to how the Hebrew scriptures were viewed at the beginning of the second century B.C.E. in Palestine. It is evident that the Torah had long since been accepted as authoritative scripture that status would receive further confirmation by the Greek translation of the Pentateuch in the third century. In addition, Ben Sira is familiar with the prophetic books and in a canonical order that knows already the unit of the twelve minor prophets (Sirach 49:10). If one leaves aside the question of the *terminus a quo* of the canonical collection of the law and the prophets on which scholars continue to differ, the evidence from Ben Sira seems to confirm a *terminus ad quem* of these two parts by 200 B.C.E.

The prologue, which the grandson of Ben Sira wrote for his Greek translation of his grandfather's Hebrew book in approximately 130 B.C.E., speaks of the "teachings which have been given us through the law and the prophets and the others that followed him." The apparent vagueness of the latter reference has traditionally been used as major evidence that the third part of the Hebrew canon had not yet been fixed at this time. Yet most recently Beckwith has warned against interpreting these words in an overly loose sense (1985:166). He notes that the prologue makes a sharp distinction between Hebrew compositions such as his grandfather's work and those contained in the three-fold Hebrew scriptures. In sum, the prologue is inconclusive in determining the extent to which the Hebrew canon was closed. It only establishes the fact that the category of Writings was still fluid within the collection of non-Mosaic books.

Usually the new Testament encompasses all of the Jewish scriptures under the rubric "law and prophets" (Acts 13:15) but in one place clearly a threefold structuring of the Old Testament appears: "the law of Moses, and the Prophets and the Psalms" (Luke 24:44; see Philo, *On the Contemplative Life* §25). It is still possible to argue that the exact scope of the Hagiographa cannot be determined from the inclusion of the Psalter even though the emphasis of the passage is on the whole of scripture and not its parts. However, when one takes the New Testament in its entirety, the impression given is clearly that of a well-defined body of authoritative scripture that includes frequent reference to late books (Daniel, Esther, Nehemiah). The debate between Jesus and the Jews concerning the interpretation of their scriptures assumed a body of writings that was held in common by both parties.

The first unequivocal evidence for the closure of the Hebrew scriptures is offered in Josephus' famous statement, about 93–95 C.E. In contrast to others who have "myriads of inconsistent books," he explicitly limits the number of sacred books to twenty-two, and enumerates a tripartite division, albeit in an order which is historically arranged and different from the Masoretic.

The earliest rabbinic evidence of a fixed collection is a *baraita* on the order of the Prophets and Writings found in the Babylonian Talmud (*b. Baba Batra* 14b). The dating of the passage is of course uncertain although Beckwith has recently argued that it is earlier than Josephus. It would be more cautious to hold that it is no later than 200 C.E. The passage assumes a fixed number of twenty-four books and a threefold division of the canon. This standard Jewish tradition continues throughout the Talmudic literature. It is further supported by a number of church Fathers (Origen [185–254], Epiphanius [315–403], Jerome [342–420]) as correctly representing the form and scope of the Jewish canon.

To summarize, it would seem that the direct literary evidence from historical sources is not sufficiently decisive to establish conclusively the scope and form of the Jewish canon at the period of the rise of Christianity. There is full agreement that the Jewish canon was closed at least by 100 C.E, but debate continues as to whether it was closed at an earlier date, indeed by the end of the first century B.C.E.

Indirect Evidence for Closure

It is at this juncture that an important additional argument has been raised in favor of an open canon throughout the first century C.E. Sundberg has argued that the highly flexible use of the Old Testament by the Christian church affords strong evidence for an open Jewish canon. He writes, "The uncertainly in the church about the extent of the Old Testament could not have arisen if the extent of the Old Testament had already been fixed in the time of Jesus and of the primitive church" (130). A similar position has been represented by Jepsen, Eissfeldt, Gese, and others.

In my opinion, there are some major reasons why this argument cannot be sustained. First of all, even from a logical point of view, one cannot necessarily deduce that the Jewish canon was unstable because the Christian church's use of it reflected a great degree of flexibility. It would seem to be a sounder methodological approach first to determine the evidence for or against first-century canonical stability from within Jewish sources themselves before seeking to explain the peculiar Christian practice. Particularly Swanson, Leiman, and Beckwith have argued for a much greater degree of textual stability within certain circles of Judaism than has been admitted by Sundberg.

The indirect evidence that supports a more stable Jewish canon at a much earlier date is as follows:

(1) Josephus' treatise *Against Apion*, which established the fixed number of the canon at twenty-two books, is usually dated about 93 C.E. On the basis of this date of composition, Josephus is thought to support the openness of the canon until the period after the "synod" of Jamnia that was envisioned as an effort of rabbinic Judaism to reconstitute their traditions following the destruction of Jerusalem. However, Josephus is reporting tradition concerning scripture long held by Jews that he had probably learned early in his life as a member of the Pharisaic party (about 56-57 C.E.). Josephus is therefore reflecting Pharisaic tradition about 50 C.E. rather than that of post-70 C.E. When one then discounts the decisive role of Jamnia, Josephus is seen to support a much earlier date

for the closure of the Jewish canon than has generally been recognized.

(2) Another major reason for assuming that the Jewish canon was still fluid until the end of the first century C.E. has been the loose reference to the Writings, the third section of the Hebrew canon (see Prologue to Sirach/Ecclesiasticus). Yet this interpretation assumes that the three sections of the Hebrew canon developed in a sequential, historical order—a position still defended in the learned essay of Hans Peter Rüger (1988)—which has been increasingly called into question. The analyses of Swanson (1970) and Beckwith (1985:142ff.) have made another option highly plausible of seeing the growth of the concept of the Hagiographa as a subsequent division within the non-Mosaic collection of the Prophets which development does not relate directly to the issue of canonical closure at all. The unbroken chain of witnesses to a Bible consisting of twenty-two scrolls from 90-400 C.E. (see Zahn 1888:336) which even allowed the books to vary but kept the number unaltered would further support the stabilization of the Jewish canon from an early period (also Katz 1956:199).

(3) The evidence that Pharisaic Judaism had a fixed form of scripture is further supported by the lack of citations from the Apocrypha in Philo, Josephus, and the New Testament. Similarly, Ben Sira, the authors of the Maccabees, Hillel, Shammai and all the first-century Tan-

naim never cite the apocryphal literature as scripture (Leiman 1976:39). Further, the evidence from the Alexandrian church Fathers of the third and fourth centuries (Origen, Athanasius) testify that the biblical canon at Alexandria consisted also of no more than twenty-two books following the Jewish tradition.

(4) The strongest evidence for a fixed Hebrew canon derives from the history of the stabilization of the Masoretic text. Material from Qumran and adjacent caves indicate that the Masoretic text had assumed a high level of stabilization by C.E. 70. Moreover, already in the first century B.C.E. a proto-Lucianic recension of the Greek Bible attempted to revise the LXX to conform to an evolving Hebrew test. Similarly the revision of the Greek in the beginning of the first century C.E. the proto-Theodotian recension, also brought the Greek into conformity with the proto-Masoretic Hebrew text (see Cross 1975). Most importantly, this recension includes the books of Daniel, Ruth, and Lamentations. The implications for the issue of the canon are clear. The text of a book would not have been corrected and stabilized if the book had not already received some sort of canonical status.

To summarize: the evidence is very strong that at least within the circles of rabbinic Judaism a concept of an established Hebrew canon with a relatively fixed scope of writings and an increasingly stabilized authoritative text had emerged by the first century B.C.E.

The Formation of the
Larger Christian Canon

In the light of this evidence how does one explain the great diversity of Jewish religious writings that were present during the period of the rise of Christianity and were shortly appropriated in various degrees by the Christian church?

One traditional way of handling the problem was to formulate the theory of an Alexandrian canon. Accordingly, the Jews in Alexandria, in distinction from those in Palestine, had a far broader canon that was a major reason for the Christian church under Greek influence to adopt a wider selection of books than Pharisaic Judaism. However, Sundberg has conclusively undermined this thesis in showing that the issue of diversity cannot be resolved by this geographical distinction.

Sundberg's own thesis, similar to that of Jepsen and Gese, is that there was a wide religious literature without definite bounds that circulated throughout Judaism prior to the decisions at Jamnia. These Jewish writings simply passed into the Christian church as a legacy from Judaism. From the great diversity of available writings, the church established for itself in time the scope of its Old Testament canon. Conversely, rabbinic Judaism, reacting to the rise of sectarianism, especially Christianity, and to the defeat from the Romans in 70 C.E., sought to reconstitute its tradition by retrenchment. It narrowed its canonical scriptures by sharply restricting the use of apocalyptic writings, by limiting the canon to writings in Hebrew, and by subordinating the whole to a dominating legal core of Torah.

However, in my opinion, there are some major problems with this reconstruction. The supporting argument of G. F. Moore—that Rabbi Akiba's ban was intended as a repudiation of Christian literature—has not been sustained (1911). Rather, the rejected books, the *sifrē minîm*, are copies of holy scripture made by heretics and having nothing to do with a Jewish reaction to Christianity (Swanson 1970:311).

Sundberg's reconstruction also fails to reckon with the very different attitudes toward scripture within Judaism of this period. The discoveries at Qumran have conclusively established the wide range of religious writings treasured by one historical community of Palestine. However, by emphasizing the element of diversity, Sundberg has failed to reckon with the element of stability and restrictiveness clearly manifested in one branch of Judaism, namely Pharisaic Judaism, whose canon was essentially established before the rise of Christianity and independently of this later challenge.

Is there another hypothesis by which to explain the elements of continuity and discontinuity between the Jews and Christians regarding

the scope of the canon? First of all, it is important to recognize that Pharisaic Judaism under-
went a profound change in status. At the time
of the rise of Christianity it represented only
one party, albeit an important one, within
Judaism, but with many rivals. However, following the debacle of 70 C.E., Pharisaism, that
is, rabbinic Judaism, not only assumed a domi-
nant historical role, but became identified with
Judaism itself from that period onward.

From the evidence of the New Testament it
seems clear that Jesus and the early Christians
identified with the scriptures of Pharisaic
Judaism. The early controversies with the Jews
reflected in the New Testament turned on the
proper interpretation of the sacred scriptures
(*hē graphē*), which Christians assumed in common with the synagogue. Although there is evidence that other books were known and used, it
is a striking fact that the New Testament does
not *cite as scripture* any book of the Apocrypha
or Pseudepigrapha. (The reference to Enoch in
Jude 14-15 is not an exception.) The use of the
Old Testament by *1 Clement* and by Justin Mar-
tyr is further confirmation of the assumption of
a common scripture between the synagogue
and the church, even if in fact a slight variation
had begun to appear.

Yet it is also evident that very soon after the
inception of the church a different attitude
toward the Jewish scriptures arose within the
church, which claimed a warrant in the tradi-

tions of Jesus' own use of scripture. The most
fundamental material change was in assigning
primary authority to Jesus Christ of whom
scripture functioned as a witness. However, in
terms of formal change, the Christian church's
adoption of the LXX in place of the original
Hebrew had immediate and profound implications respecting the canon. Increasingly, Christians abandoned the strictures of rabbinic
Judaism such as limiting canonical authority to
Hebrew writings. It is also clear that the use of
the LXX quickly eroded the limitations on the
scope of the Hebrew canon that rabbinic
Judaism had established. The Latin Bible only
further distanced the Western church from its
Jewish legacy. In spite of the fact that a knowledge of the restricted scope of the Jewish canon
was present and even authoritative within certain Christian circles, very shortly a wide diversity of opinion regarding the scope of the Old
Testament was reflected in Christianity.

Alfred Jepsen has mounted a very strong
historical case that each province of the Christian church tended to form its own canon
(1949:69-70). He demonstrated that in the East
four major forms of the Old Testament canon
can be identified according to geographical
areas. In Asia Minor the Jewish canon was recognized as scripture with the exception of
Esther. Athanasius (296-373) from Egypt like-
wise accepted the Jewish canon without Esther,
but sanctioned for public reading without the

status of scripture Wisdom, Sirach, Esther, Tobit, and Judith. In Palestine a diversity of opinion prevailed. Nicephorus and Canon 60 of the Council of Laodicea followed Athanasius in accepting the Jewish canon and allowing the public reading of certain apocryphal books to which the Maccabees was added. Other circles in Palestine had a somewhat different list of books permitted for public reading. However, in Syria the books that were allowed to be read were fully accepted as scripture in addition to the Jewish canon. The Western church followed the lead of Syria in accepting a wider canon. The synods of Hippo (393) and Carthage (397) gave this position ecclesiastical sanction in North Africa which decision influenced Rome. Finally the Council of Trent (1545–63) adopted this position definitively for the Roman church.

It seems clear that two major attitudes toward the Jewish canon have prevailed in the Christian church throughout much of its history. The one approach opting for a narrow canon identified the Christian Old Testament in terms of the literary scope and textual form of the synagogue's Hebrew canon. The other chose a wider canon and supplemented the Hebrew canon with other books that had long been treasured by parts of the church. The classic defender of the narrower canon among the church Fathers was Jerome. His counterpart as a defender of the wider canon was, of course, Augustine. The Reformation churches sided with Jerome in varying degrees, the Roman Catholic Church with Augustine. The Orthodox Church long equivocated, but increasingly sided with the wider Christian canon (see Jugie 1904). In sum, the exact nature of the Christian Bible both in respect to its scope and text remains undecided up to this day.

The Theological Problems at Stake

In the light of the proceeding historical sketch of the formation of the Christian Bible, it is evident that important theological issues are at stake that go far beyond a historical description of the disagreement. Frequently the complexity of the theological issues has been overlooked when the defenders of each position have offered a simple solution to resolve the problem.

The defenders of the narrow canon, especially those of the Reformed persuasion, have often argued that the church's confusion in opting for a wider canon arose out of an understandable error. Because the early church soon lost its knowledge of the Hebrew language and resorted to translations, it moved away from the narrow Jewish canon used by Jesus and Paul, and absorbed from the LXX a collection of non-canonical books (see Filson 1957:73-100; Metzger 1987). Conversely the defenders of the wider canon have usually argued that the LXX was the Bible of the church close to its inception and that the actual use of a wider collection of sacred books, often in translated form, provided a traditional warrant for the recognition of a Christian Bible that differs markedly from the Jewish synagogue (so Sundberg 1964). In my opinion, the theological issues at stake are much more complex than either side has acknowledged and calls for renewed theological reflection.

At the outset, it is crucial to recognize that the Christian understanding of canon functions theologically in a very different way from Judaism. Although the church adopted from the synagogue a concept of scripture as an authoritative collection of sacred writings, its basic stance toward its canon was shaped by its Christology. The authority assigned to the apostolic witnesses derived from their unique testimony to the life, death, and resurrection of Jesus Christ. Similarly, the Old Testament functioned as Christian scripture because it bore witness to Christ. The scriptures of the Old and the New Testament were authoritative in so far as they pointed to God's redemptive intervention for the world in Jesus Christ. The church Fathers, Schoolmen, and Reformers were all agreed on this basic understanding of the Bible, although obviously differing in emphases and clarity of formulation.

Within this broad theological framework, two different principles appear to have been at work throughout the history of the church. On the one hand, there was the basic concern that the truth of the apostolic witness be preserved. The attempt to distinguish between the apostolic writings and later ecclesiastical tradition lay at the heart of the formation of the Christian canon. The development of the canonical criterion of apostolicity in the selection of New Testament books was a direct application of this concern. Both the effort to guarantee the proper scope of the sacred writings and to preserve the biblical text from corruption arose from this commitment to guard the truth of the witness. Although the church was in an external, formal sense the vehicle of the sacred tradition, there was a universally acknowledged belief that God was the source of its truth and that human writers were divinely inspired by God's Spirit to bear a truthful witness. Thus the post-apostolic church strove correctly to acknowledge as authoritative those writings that were from God. Although historically the decision of the church actively shaped the canon, the church itself envisioned its task as one of acknowledging what God had given as a gracious gift in Christ for the nourishing of the continuing life of faith.

This concern to preserve the truth of the biblical witness expressed itself in regard to the Old Testament by the insistence of Jerome and others on the priority of the Hebrew canon also for the Christian Bible. He argued that the word of God to Israel had been best preserved in the Hebrew scriptures on which the various translations had been dependent and from which they had often strayed. Equally important was

the theological argument that the Jews had
been given the "covenant . . . the law, the worship, and the promises" (Romans 1:4) and were
the proper tridents of this tradition. Moreover,
Paul had also made the argument of the soli-
darity between Christ and the patriarchs from
whose "race and according to the flesh" Jesus
stemmed (Romans 9:5). Therefore to use a different collection of Old Testament writings
from those accepted by the Jews appeared as a
threat to the theological continuity of the people of God. Had not Clement and Justin based
their argument on the identity of the God of the
Old Testament with the Father of Jesus Christ
on an assumption of a common scripture
between church and synagogue?

On the other hand, an equally strong voice
was sounded placing its primary emphasis on
the catholicity of the Christian faith that was
expressed in an unbroken continuity of sacred
tradition from its risen Lord to his church. The
Christian canon arose as various writings were
experienced and acknowledged as divinely
inspired through the actual use of Christian
communities. The church Fathers used as a
major criterion by which to determine a book's
authority the testimony of the most ancient
congregations having a claim to historical continuity with the earliest apostolic tradition and
representing the most inclusive geographical
testimony of the universal church (see Augustine, *On Christian Doctrine*). Indeed it was the

larger Christian canon, particularly as represented in the Vulgate, which served as the Christian Bible for the Western church during a period of over a thousand years.

Equally important as a warrant for a uniquely Christian Bible was the practice of the biblical writers themselves. The New Testament is deeply stamped by its widespread use of the LXX. Moreover, it has long been observed that the New Testament pattern of prophecy-fulfillment frequently functions only in terms of the Greek text. Although the New Testament does not actually cite the Apocrypha as scripture—some scholars vigorously contest this point—there is some evidence pointing to a knowledge of these books by various biblical authors, especially Paul (see Aland 1968; Rüger 1988). Above all, the New Testament writers bore witness to Jesus Christ by transforming the Old Testament in a way that often stood in much tension with the original sense of the Hebrew text. If the New Testament used such freedom in respect to its Jewish heritage, does not the Christian church have a similar right to develop its own form of scripture in a manner different from that of the synagogue?

In response to these two sets of arguments, it seems necessary at the outset to recognize the uncertainty that has remained in the church regarding the form of the Christian Bible. Moreover, this diversity should be respected. Yet what is needed is not just an expedient compromise in

the name of ecumenicity, but a genuine theological grappling with the issues that is prepared to test the strengths and weaknesses of
both traditional positions. To insist that the
problems demand a theological solution is to
reject as inadequate all biblicist approaches,
whether emerging from the left or right of the
theological spectrum. Every practice of the
early church cannot be simply copied by successive generations of Christians. The fact that
the New Testament writers employed Hellenistic techniques of exegesis such as allegory and
midrash is no warrant *per se* for their continu-
ance. Nor can one argue for the continuing
authoritative role of a Greek or Latin translation merely because of its early use. Underlying
this argument is an appeal for a "kerygmatic,"
that is, christological reading of scripture rather
than a biblicist one.

It is also important that the proper dimensions of the issue of the Christian Bible be kept
in focus. Because the outer limits of the Christian canon remained unsettled, or because the
role of translations was assessed differently
among various groups of Christians, the conclu-
sion cannot be drawn that the church has functioned without a scripture or in deep confusion.
Rather, the implication to be drawn is exactly
the reverse. In spite of areas of disagreement, the
Bible in its various forms has continued to function as an authoritative norm for the church
throughout its history. Nor can one discern a

great change in its function when, for example, the Apocrypha was included in the Geneva Bible, but then removed from the Authorized Version (KJV) in the nineteenth century.

The great strength of the Reformers' returning to the narrower Hebrew canon of the Old Testament lay in their concern to establish the truth of the biblical witness according to its most pristine and purest form. The priority of scripture over church tradition arose from the conviction that the object of the witness, namely God's revelation in Jesus Christ, provided the critical norm by which to test the truth of its reception. God himself testified to its truth by inspiring both the authors and readers of the sacred writings. Yet the history of the post-Reformation church also illustrates the weakness of the Reformers' use of a critical norm and of its insufficiency in practice. It would be difficult to argue, for example, that the elimination of the Apocrypha from the Protestant Bible derived solely from the working of the inner testimony of the Holy Spirit. Or was a material principle clear enough to distinguish so sharply between the miracles of the Hebrew Daniel and the Greek Daniel (see Reuss 1891:312)?

The Roman Catholic insistence upon the decisive role of tradition in shaping the Christian Bible correctly recognized the role of the church's actual use of its scripture both in proclamation and liturgy. The church's practice of worship provided the context in which the biblical message was received, treasured, and transmitted. The church's rule-of-faith, later expressed in creeds, did not seek to impose an alien ecclesiastical tradition upon the scriptures, but rather sought to preserve the unity of word and tradition as the Spirit continually enlivened the truth of the gospel from which the church lived. However, the danger of the Catholic position that emerged in the course of the church's history lay in the temptation to render the Word captive to more easily adaptable human traditions, often in the name of piety. Any appeal solely to tradition or praxis apart form the critical norm exercised by the content of the biblical witness eventually runs counter to the essence of a Christian theology of canon.

Perhaps the basic theological issue at stake can be best formulated in terms of the church's ongoing *search* for the Christian Bible. The church struggles with the task of continually discerning the truth of God being revealed in scripture and at the same time she stands within a fully human, ecclesiastical tradition that remains the tradent of the Word. The hearing of God's Word is repeatedly confirmed by the Holy Spirit through its resonance with the church's christological rule-of-faith. At the same time the church confesses the inadequacy of its reception while rejoicing over the sheer wonder of the divine accommodations to limited human capacity.

Part of the task of a Biblical Theology is to participate in the search for the Christian Bible. The enterprise is not one that will be resolved once-and-for-all, but one which appears to be constitutive for Christian faith. The dialectical poles, historically represented by the Protestant and Catholic positions, chart the arena between Word and Tradition that is reflected in the controversy over the extent of the Christian canon. Equally important is the critical tension between the form and the substance of the church's witness in scripture that calls for a continual struggle for truthful interpretation. One of the purposes of this attempt at a Biblical Theology is to apply these hermeneutical guidelines in working theologically within the narrow and wider forms of the canon in search for both the truth and the catholicity of the biblical witness to the church and the world.

In sum, the proposal being made is not that of developing a canon-within-the-canon, nor is it of identifying the canon with accumulated ecclesiastical tradition. Rather, the complete canon of the Christian church as the rule-of-faith sets for the community of faith the proper theological context in which we stand, but it also remains continually the object of critical theological scrutiny subordinate to its subject matter who is Jesus Christ. This movement from the outer parameters of tradition to the inner parameters of Word is constitutive of the theological task.

3
A Canonical Approach
to Biblical Theology

The purpose of this chapter is to describe how concern for the hermeneutical implications of the Christian canon affects the way in which one envisions the task of Biblical Theology.

A Canonical Approach to the Two Testaments

In my two previous Introductions to the Old Testament and to the New Testament, I have tried to describe the effect of the role of the canon on the formation of each of the testaments. A major point that emerged was the insight that the lengthy process of the development of the literature leading up to the final stage of canonization involved a profoundly hermeneutical activity on the part of the tridents (*contra* Barr 1983:67). The material was transmitted through its various oral, literary, and redactional stages by many different groups toward a theological end. Because the traditions were received as religiously authoritative, they were transmitted in such a way as to maintain a normative function for subsequent generations of believers within a community of faith. This process of rendering the material theologically involved countless different compositional techniques by means of which the tradition was actualized.

In my description of this process I used the term "canonical" as a cipher to encompass the various and diverse factors involved in the formation of the literature. The term was, above all, useful in denoting the reception and acknowledgment of certain religious traditions as authoritative writings within a faith community. The term also included the process by which the collection arose which led up to its final stage of literary and textual stabilization, that is, canonization proper. Emphasis was placed on the process to demonstrate that the concept of canon was not a late, ecclesiastical ordering which was basically foreign to the material itself, but that canon-consciousness lay deep within the formation of the literature. The term also serves to focus attention on the theological forces at work in its composition rather than seeking the process largely controlled by general laws of folklore, by sociopolitical factors, or by scribal conventions.

I also included in the term "canonical" an important addition component that was a theological extension of its primary meaning.

The canonical form of this literature also affects how the modern reader understands the biblical material, especially to the extent in which he or she identifies religiously with the faith community of the original tridents. The modern theological function of canon lies in its affirmation that the authoritative norm lies in the literature itself as it has been treasured, transmitted and transformed—of course in constant relation to its object to which it bears witness—and not in "objectively" reconstructed stages of the process. The term "canon" points to the received, collected, and interpreted material of the church and thus establishes the theological context in which the tradition continues to function authoritatively for today.

Canonical Text or Canonical Interpreter?

One of the main endeavors of my two Introductions was to describe the manner by which the hermeneutical concerns of the tridents left their mark on the literature. The material was shaped in order to provide means for its continuing appropriation by its subsequent hearers. Guidelines were given which rendered the material compatible with its future actualization. For example, in the Old Testament the Book of Deuteronomy, which arose historically in the late monarchial period of Israel's history, was assigned a particular canonical function as

It will remain useful for the church

interpreter of the law by its structure and position within the Pentateuch (Childs 1979: 211-13). Or again, in the New Testament the Gospel of Luke was separated from Acts with which it was originally formed, and given a new context and role within the fourfold Gospel collection (Childs 1985:116). I also stressed in this description of the canonical shaping the enormous variety at work on the different levels of composition. This shaping activity functioned much like a *regula fidei* (rule of faith). It was a negative criterion that set certain parameters within which the material functioned, but largely left to exegesis the positive role of interpretation within the larger construal.

Ever since I first proposed this understanding of the significance of canon a decade and a half ago, there have been a variety of critical responses from within the biblical guild. Perhaps one of the more characteristic criticisms has recently been reiterated by Walter Brueggemann (1991). He is representative of a number of biblical scholars who have not rejected the canonical proposal out-of-hand like James Barr (1983), but who have sought to improve on it with certain alterations. Brueggemann makes the following points:

(1) Childs has asserted a theological claim for canon by means of a purely literary, formal argument expressed in terms of shaping of the text, whereas the claim of authority should have been made in terms of theological content.

(2) It is not the biblical text that is the decisive tradent of the theological norm, but the activity of the interpreter who as the "canonical interpreter" is engaged in the continuing process of actualizing the text to recover the liberating concerns of God.

(3) The social reality expressed by the oppressed on the margins of society gives voice to the basic theological substance which undergirds biblical authority, and canonical interpretation is the open-ended conversation with the disenfranchised, which reclaims biblical truth from all false claims of authority and power of the establishment.

In response I would argue that to suggest my approach to canon is a purely formal, literary construct without theological content is a fundamental misunderstanding of the proposal. The whole point of focusing on scripture as canon in opposition to the anthropocentric tradition of liberal Protestantism is to emphasize that the biblical text and its theological function as authoritative form belong inextricably together. A major danger in the traditional Catholic discussion of canon, to which the Reformers were particularly sensitive (Calvin, *Institutes* 1.7.3), was that canon not be interpreted as an extrinsic ecclesiastical norm, independent and superior in authority to the biblical text itself. Therefore, their insistence was that the text itself renders the proper scope of scripture that the church only receives and acknowledges.

It is ironic after this initial attack that Brueggemann immediately falls into this very theological trap of separating text and norm. For the canonical text he substitutes the neutral term "classic" (Brueggemann 1991:121), appealing to the terminology of David Tracy, which refers to any text within a community which functions as a vehicle for establishing identity by evoking claims to attention (Tracy 1981:102). One hears no more of canon as the unique Apostolic witness to the gospel in response to which the worshiping community in prayer, repentance, and anticipation awaits a quickening of the Spirit through a living word of God.

Rather, and crucial to Brueggemann's proposal, is his defining those forces in human society which activate the classic into a contextualized norm. The inert text of the classic receives its meaning when it is correlated with some other external cultural force, ideology, or mode of existence. Of course, this is exactly the hermeneutical typology that Hans Frei so brilliantly described in his book, *The Eclipse of Biblical Narrative* (1973). It makes little difference whether the needed component for correctly interpreting the Bible is the Enlightenment's appeal to reason, consciousness, and pure spirit, or to Karl Marx's anti-Enlightenment ideology of a classless society and the voice of the proletariat. The hermeneutical move is identical. Brueggemann's attraction to Gottwald's thesis derives from the latter's providing a quasi-Marxist analysis of an alleged social reality lying behind the text which he can identify with the prophetic voice of the Bible. The result is fully predictable. The theological appeal to an authoritative canonical text that has been shaped by Israel's witness to a history of divine, redemptive intervention has been replaced by a radically different construal. The saddest part of the proposal is that Walter Brueggemann is sincerely striving to be a confessing theologian of the Christian church, and would be horrified at being classified as a most eloquent defender of the Enlightenment, which his proposal respecting the biblical canon actually represents.

Canonical Shaping and the Two Testaments of the Christian Bible

If one were to characterize the nature of the shaping within the two testaments, it could initially be described in a formal sense as a literary or redactional layering of the text that developed through a transmission process. Often old material has been given a new redactional framework (the Book of Judges, for example), or an interpretive commentary added (Ecclesiastes), or originally separate literary entities combined into a single composition (Philippians). There are also a few examples within both testaments in which there is no sign of explicit redactional layering, but a new way of reading the literature has emerged from the larger canonical context (Daniel, Romans).

Now a crucial question immediately arises when one attempts to apply the same canonical approach that was used in relation to the individual testaments to the Christian Bible as a whole. In what sense can one speak of the canonical shaping of the Christian Bible when the process by which the two testaments were joined appears to be quite different from that reflected in each of the individual testaments? It is to this problem we now turn.

The juxtaposition of the two testaments to form the Christian Bible arose, not simply to establish a historical continuity between Israel and the church, but above all as an affirmation of a theological continuity. The church not only joined its new writings to the Jewish scriptures, but laid claim on the Old Testament as a witness to Jesus Christ. A variety of different theological moves were made by which to articulate the theological relationship of the two dispensations: the one purpose of God, the one redemptive history (or story), the one people of God, prophecy and fulfillment, law and gospel, shadow and substance, etc. No one theological interpretation of the relationship became absolute for Christian theology, but the simple juxtaposition of the two testaments as the two parts of the one Bible continued to allow for a rich theological diversity. The subsequent christological debates during the first centuries of the church's life ruled out certain options as heretical which either denigrated the Old Testament as an unworthy witness to Christ (Marcion, Gnostics), or relegated the New Testament to a subordinate position within the structures of Judaism (Ebionism).

There are, however, certain signs of Christian redactional activity in the reordering of the Hebrew scriptures when it was appropriated as the Old Testament of the church. It is immediately apparent that the tripartite division of the Masoretic text (Torah, Prophets, Writings) has been disregarded in the Christian Bible. It has been replaced with an order that begins with the Pentateuch (Law), but then joins the various historical books together, followed by wisdom and hymnody, and concludes with the prophetic books. The problem of this different arrangement of the Old Testament is more complex than it once appeared. First, it is historically inaccurate to assume that the present printed forms of the Hebrew Bible and of the Christian Bible represent ancient and completely fixed traditions. Actually the present stability regarding the ordering of the books is to a great extent dependent on modern printing techniques and carries no significant theological weight. For example, the form, say, of Gerhard Kittel's *Biblia Hebraica* is not identical with that represented in the Talmud. Similarly, the sequence of the Christian Old Testament varied greatly in the earliest lists of the church

Fathers. In sum, the importance of the different orders should not be overestimated.

By and large, one can say that the form of the tripartite division of the Hebrew Bible was not absolutely fixed in Jewish tradition during the first centuries of the Christian era and was in a state of some fluidity at the rise of Christianity. The main point is that the Masoretic text does not represent the oldest established pattern that was then subsequently altered by Christians. Rather, there were many competing traditions in the pre-Christian period equally ancient, some of which are reflected in the various sequences of the Greek Bible. The Christian church did not create its own order *de novo,* but rather selected from available options an order that best reflected its new, evangelical understanding of the Hebrew scriptures. Specifically this means that the prophets were relegated to the end of the collection as pointing to the coming of the promised Messiah. It is also possible to see some theological intentionality in the regrouping of the historical books. The effect was to designate the old covenant with Israel as a historical period in the past that retained its revelatory value, but to see the ongoing continuity in the prophetic word rather than in the historical continuity of the nation Israel. Still caution is in order not to overestimate the conscious theological intentionality of these changes (*contra* Preuss 1984). Equally as significant is the resulting effect of these changes in the ordering on the reading of the literature even when fortuitous elements were clearly involved.

A most striking feature in the juxtaposition of the two testaments is actually the lack of Christian redactional activity on the Old Testament. Although the post-apostolic church tended to expand the number of the books of the Old Testament in relation to the Hebrew canon (see above:chap. 2 for the problem of the Apocrypha), the shape of the books in the Jewish canon was left largely unchanged. There was no attempt made to christianize the Old Testament through redactional changes, for example, by bracketing the Old Testament books with parts of the Gospels, or by adding Christian commentary, features which are present in both the apocryphal and pseudepigraphical literature. Rather the collection of Jewish scriptures was envisioned as closed and a new and different collection began which in time evolved into the New Testament.

The question at issue then is whether one can still talk of "canonical shaping" in relation to the Christian Bible when there is no analogy to the multilayering activity of tridents who were continually at work in the individual testaments bringing the authoritative writings into conformity with a larger canonical intentionality. In response to this problem, at first it seemed to me best to turn to the composition of the fourfold Gospel collection as providing the closest analogy to the relation of the two testaments. One of the major characteristics of this Gospel collection was also precisely its lack of redactional activity. With a few minor exceptions (Childs 1985:143–56), the four Gospels were simply juxtaposed without an attempt to make the individual books conform to a single redactional pattern. Naturally the juxtaposition of the four Gospels caused a strong effect on the reader because of the new and larger context created in spite of the lack of a single editorial intentionality. Could one then press the analogy of the fourfold Gospel collection with the Christian Bible as a whole because of the lack of an intentional redactional direction and see the hermeneutical importance to lie in the resulting effect of the juxtaposition?

There is, however, a major difference between these two collections comprising the fourfold Gospels and the two part Christian Bible which is so striking as to call into question any close analogy. The four Gospels have been formed into a collection without any inner cross-referencing. Although there is much common material among the Gospels, and even a close literary relationship of dependency among the Synoptics, the Gospels themselves never make explicit reference to each other. Even the prologue of Luke is no exception. In contrast, each of the individual Gospels—albeit in different ways—makes constant and explicit reference to the Old Testament. Indeed, the use of the Old

Testament performs a major role in the canonical shaping of each of the Gospels and many of the New Testament letters as well.

There is an important implication to be drawn from this situation. The influence of the Old Testament on the individual shaping of the Gospels belongs to the level of the New Testament's compositional history and cannot be directly related to the formation of the Christian Bible *as* collection. This means that the New Testament's use of the Old Testament, either by direct citation or allusion, cannot provide a central category for Biblical Theology because this cross-referencing operates on a different level. There is no literary or theological warrant for assuming that the forces that shaped the New Testament can be simply extended to the level of Biblical Theology involving theological reflection on both testaments. In this regard, my earliest attempt at using New Testament citations of the Old Testament as a major category for Biblical Theology stands in need of revision and is an inadequate handling of the problem (Childs 1970:114 ff.).

There are two further hermeneutical implications—both negative—to be drawn from the peculiar juxtaposing of the two testaments. The first addresses those biblical theologians who would overstress the continuity between the two testaments. Because the New Testament is not a redactional layer on the Old Testament, and is not to be seen as an analogy to the

Chronicler's editing of the Book of Kings, it is inaccurate to speak of a unified traditio-historical trajectory which links the two testaments in unbroken continuity (*contra* Gese 1970). Nor can one rightly envision the New Testament as a midrashic extension of the Hebrew scriptures that stands in closest analogy to rabbinic and Qumran exegesis. The canonical continuity established by the shape of the Christian Bible is of a different order.

The second implication addresses those who stress the discontinuity between the testaments, such as Rudolf Bultmann and his school. Because "Christ is the end of the law," the relation between the testaments has been largely characterized as negative. The Old Testament is a testimony to miscarriage and failure. However, again the canonical shaping of the two testaments provides no warrant for such a judgment. Indeed the Jewish scriptures have been designated as "Old Testament," but not in the sense of failure and rejection. Rather the canonical relationship is far more complex. The Old is understood by its relation to the New, but the New is incomprehensible apart from the Old. Exactly how this traditional formation functions for Biblical Theology will require a more detailed exposition.

Canonical Guidelines for Structuring Biblical Theology

Our concern up to this juncture has been to explore for Biblical Theology the hermeneutical implications of the form that the canon has given the Christian Bible. Emphasis has fallen on the unity of the one composition consisting of two separate testaments. The two testaments have been linked as Old and New, but this designation does not mean that the integrity of each individual testament has been destroyed. The Old Testament bears its true witness as the Old that remains distinct from the New. It is promise, not fulfillment. Yet its voice continues to sound and it has not been stilled by the fulfillment of the promise.

The significance of emphasizing the continuing canonical integrity of the Old Testament lies in resisting the Christian temptation to identify Biblical Theology with the New Testament's interpretation of the Old, as if the Old Testament's witness were limited to how it was once heard and appropriated by the early church. One of the major objections to the Tübingen form of Biblical Theology (Gese, Stuhlmacher) is that the Old Testament has become a horizontal stream of tradition from the past whose witness has been limited to its effect on subsequent writers. The Old Testament has thus lost its vertical, existential dimension that as scripture of the church continues to bear its own witness within the context of the Christian Bible.

Recently Hans Hübner has defended the thesis that it is only the Old Testament as received by the New Testament that is authoritative for the Christian church and appropriate for biblical reflection (1990:18–19). In a separate article I have attempted to show in some detail why such an approach destroys the theological integrity of the Old Testament and silences its true canonical witness (Childs 1992).

Another important reason for distinguishing the task of Biblical Theology from the new Testament's use of the Old is that the modern Christian theologian shares a different canonical context for the early church. The first Christian writers had only one testament, the modern Christian has two. Although there is an obvious analogy between the early church's reinterpretation of the Jewish scripture in the light of the Gospel and the modern church's use of two authoritative testaments, the fact of the Christian Bible consisting of two testaments distinguishes the task of Biblical Theology from that of New Testament theology. Both testaments make a discrete witness to Jesus Christ that must be heard, both separately and in concert.

At the heart of the problem of Biblical Theology lies the issue of doing full justice to the subtle canonical relationship of the two testaments within the one Christian Bible. On the one hand, the Christian canon asserts the continuing integrity of the Old Testament witness. It must be heard on its own terms. The problem with traditional Christian allegory was its refusal to hear the Old Testament's witness, and to change its semantic level in order to bring it into conformity with the New Testament.

On the other hand, the New Testament makes its own witness. It tells its own story of the new redemptive intervention of God in Jesus Christ. The New Testament is not just an extension of the Old, nor a last chapter in an epic tale. Something totally new has entered in the gospel. Yet the complexity of the problem arises because the New Testament bears its totally new witness in terms of the old, and thereby transforms the Old Testament. Frequently the Old Testament is heard on a different level from its original or literal sense, and in countless figurative ways it reinterprets the Old to testify to Jesus Christ. This description is not to suggest that the plain sense of the Old Testament is always disregarded by the New Testament, but only that the New Testament most characteristically comes to the Old Testament from the perspective of the gospel and freely renders the Old as a transparency of the New.

As a result, a major task of Biblical Theology is to reflect on the whole Christian Bible with its two very different voices, both of which the church confesses bear witness to Jesus Christ. There is no one overarching hermeneutical theory by which to resolve the tension between the testimony of the Old Testament in its own right and that of the New Testament with its transformed Old Testament. Yet the challenge of Biblical Theology is to engage in the continual activity of theological reflection that studies the canonical text in detailed exegesis, and seeks to do justice to the witness of both testaments in the light of its subject matter who is Jesus Christ. It is to this move from the Bible as witness, to the subject matter of the witness, that we next turn.

4

From Witness
to Subject Matter

Up to now the emphasis for reconstituting Biblical Theology has fallen on the need for such an
enterprise of biblical interpretation to hear the
different voices of both testaments in their
canonical integrity. Yet a fundamental problem
immediately emerges when the New Testament's
use of the Old Testament cannot be easily recon-
ciled with the Old Testament's own witness. Traditional Christianity sought to overcome the
problem by harmonizing the difficulties. More
recently, a variety of biblical theological solu-
tions have been proposed, either by subordinating the Old Testament to the New, by an
appeal to some form of *Heilsgeschichte* ("salvation history"), or by massive theological
reductionism.

Theories of Access
to the Subject Matter

A major thesis of this book is that this basic
problem in Biblical Theology can only be
resolved by theological reflection which moves

from a description of the biblical witness to the object toward which these witnesses point, that is, to their subject matter, substance, or *res*. Yet to make this suggestion is to plunge Biblical Theology into an arena of problems with which dogmatic theology has been struggling since its inception. What does one mean by subject matter or substance? What is the relation of this reality to the biblical texts? How does one discern this reality and what are its characteristics? The question can well be posed: why increase the problem of Biblical Theology by linking it again to such complex theological and philosophical issues? How does it help the discipline of Biblical Theology? Is this not once again to be entrapped by Aristotle?

First of all, the proposal to raise these issues brings into the foreground of the discussion a fundamental problem that has either been pushed into the background or consigned to an interpreter's hidden agenda. Seldom has the issue of the substance of the witness, that is, its reality, been dealt with above board and clearly, but rather some sort of assumed hermeneutic has been silently operative. A few examples will suffice to make the point.

(1) Gerhard von Rad's form of *Heilsgeschichte* as a history of continual actualization of tradition assumes that there is a reality lying behind the various witnesses which emerges in ever greater clarity at the end of the process, but which can also at times be anticipated

through typological adumbration. Yet the reader is given only vague hints of what is theologically involved. In his final chapter (1965:319ff.) von Rad is forced to fall back to several traditional, but often conflicting, schemata (Law/Gospel, prophecy/fulfillment, letter/spirit) in order to relate the Old Testament's substance to his christological model (see Oeming 1987:58ff.).

(2) Rudolf Bultmann's search for the reality behind the New Testament's witness assumes it to be a mode of authentic existence that is described by means of modern existentialist categories (1951–55). Only those New Testament writers who appear compatible to this move provide vehicles for an authentic voice (Paul, John) while many other New Testament authors are rendered largely mute by means of critical deconstruction (Luke, Pastorals, 2 Peter, Revelation).

(3) Paul Tillich speaks freely of the reality of the New Being that conquers existential estrangement and makes faith possible. Jesus as the Christ is the symbolic expression of this New Being, and the biblical portrait of this symbol mediates a knowledge of God. Participation, not historical argument, guarantees the event on which faith is grounded as a sign of the continuing transforming power of this reality once encountered by Jesus' disciples. That the Old Testament plays a minor role is apparently taken for granted.

(4) Again, many modern "narrative theologies" seek to avoid all dogmatic issues in the study of the Bible and seek "to render reality" only by means of retelling the story. (Hence the agreement of both liberals and conservatives regarding the centrality of narrative, but who disagree concerning the nature of the "old, old story".) The move has recently become popular of inviting the reader to enter the fictive world of the biblical text, a realm of symbolic language, which evokes new imagery for its hearers. Clearly an assumption is being made regarding the nature and function of the Bible that privileges the genre of story over against those other biblical forms of psalmody, law, and wisdom.

(5) Finally, many modern biblical scholars have been attracted by a hermeneutical theory such as that proposed by David Kelsey (1980), who defends the position that the Bible's authority does not rest on any specific content or property of the text, but lies in the function to which biblical patterns have been assigned by the imaginative construals of a community of faith. One cannot rightly attack the consistency of the theory, but the theological issue turns on whether one can do justice to the function of scripture when it is so loosely related to its subject matter, that is, to its reality.

Yet to speak of a reality in some form not identical with the biblical text as the grounds for theological reflection raises for many the specter of a return to static dogmatic categories of the past. Thomas Aquinas assumed an analogy of being between divine and human reality that could be discerned to some degree by means of reason. Both the Reformers and the philosophers of the Enlightenment resisted strongly any direct move from general being to a sure knowledge of God, and such a move finds few modern defenders. A repristination of any form of traditional ontology seems out of the question for multiple reasons. Clearly the crucial issue in any appeal to the substance of the biblical witness turns on how the term is defined and how the biblical reality is understood.

At this juncture, Gerhard Ebeling is helpful in his contrasting the philosophical use of the term *substantia* with that of the Bible. The term in its classic philosophical form denotes "the essence of a thing, the *ipsa essentia rei*, its *quidditas* in distinction from its accidents and qualities, which is ontologically conceived . . . In contrast, the term *substantia* means in Scripture not the essence of a thing, but what reality means for human beings who are involved with it and who understand themselves in relation to it" (1971:24).

Ebeling's definition is helpful in contrasting the biblical understanding with the impersonal conceptions of divine substance of Western philosophy. However, the question can be raised whether Ebeling has described the biblical alternative too much in modern existential

categories. I would rather argue that the reality
of God cannot be defined within any kind of
foundationalist categories and then transferred
to God. Rather it is crucial that the reality of
God be understood as primary. Moreover,
according to the Bible the reality of God has no
true being apart from communion, first within
God's self, and secondly with his creation. God
is one whose being is in loving which is
grounded in a freely given commitment toward
humanity and this relationship is constitutive
of his being (see Torrance 1989:352ff.). Therefore, in spite of the danger of misconstruing
such theological terminology, it seems difficult
to avoid when reflecting theologically on this
dimension of the Bible.

The problem of definition only confirms the
point that the decisive task of Biblical Theology
lies in giving the terminology theological content. It is a misleading caricature offered by
some biblical scholars to suggest that any concern for biblical reality must end up with a static deposit, a "ground of being," or an abstraction
of timeless ideals. Whatever theological decisions are made respecting method must finally
be tested by their ability to do justice to this pro-
foundest dimension of the Christian Bible. To
offer only one example: the Old Testament witness to creation does not ever sound the name of
Jesus. At the same time, it is equally true that the
Old Testament does not conceive of the creator
God as a monad or monolithic block. In Genesis,

in the prophets, and especially in the wisdom books, there is a dynamic activity within the Godhead and an eschatological relation between the old and the new, between creation once-for-all and *creatio continua* ("on-going creation"), between divine transcendence and immanent entrance into the world. It is crucial for any serious Christian theology to reflect on how this variety of witness to the God of Israel is to be understood in the light of the New Testament's witness (John, Colossians, Hebrews) to the creative role of Jesus Christ in relation to the Father. It is my thesis that such reflection demands a continuing wrestling with the central issue of the reality constitutive of these biblical witnesses.

Redefining the Subject Matter of the Biblical Witness

Perhaps the logical place to begin in order to give the problem of the substance of the biblical witness a more precise formulation is with the hermeneutical issue at stake in this proposal.

(1) There is general agreement among modern critical interpreters of the Bible that exegesis involves, above all, a descriptive task of hearing each biblical text in its own integrity which includes exact philosophical, historical, and literary analysis. Yet the exegetical enterprise goes beyond mere description and

addresses the content testified by the witness. Some interpreters, who take a lead from Wilhelm Dilthey, have attempted to distinguish two stages within the enterprise. They designate the scientific analysis of the text according to the above-mentioned use of critical tools as *erklären*, whereas the term *verstehen* is relegated to the effort to penetrate to the content of the witness by means of the versatility inherent in the language itself (see Luz 1985:20). The question can be raised whether this distinction is helpful. However, the main point is that the full dimension of critical exegesis be maintained and that the exegetical task not be limited to mere description. In my own opinion, *erklären* [explaining] and *verstehen* [understanding] should not be seen as two separate and distinct stages, but two parts of the one enterprise that remain dialogically related.

(2) The issue of the relation between "explanation" and "understanding" in exegesis is, however, even more complex. Recent redactional criticism has shown that often a biblical text has been subsequently interpreted within a literary framework that has the effect of reinterpreting the text in a manner different from its original meaning. In other words, a later redactor has interpreted the text according to a different referent, that is, according to another understanding of its reality. One thinks, for example, of the later redactional framework constituting Isaiah 6–9 that now interprets the term Immanuel in a highly messianic fashion,

which was not clear in the earliest levels of the tradition (see Isaiah 7:14). Or again, from the Synoptic Gospels, one often finds the redactor placing an original tradition concerning the earthly Jesus within a later framework that now understands Jesus as the exalted Christ. The task of critical exegesis involves a careful analysis of the relation of both levels of the text's witness, but also an analysis of the effect of the redacted text on its understanding of the referent(s).

(3) A further extension of this same exegetical problem is encountered in the New Testament's use of the Old. The New Testament writers bear testimony to the gospel as the revelation of God in Jesus Christ. They often return to interpret the Old Testament in the light of an understanding shaped by this exalted Christ. Especially in the case of the Apostle Paul, the author reinterprets the texts of the Old Testament according to a christological reality that renders the Old Testament in a manner at times different from its original Old Testament meaning. As a result, scholars differ greatly in their evaluation of Paul's exegesis. If an interpreter sees the exegetical task as largely descriptive (*erklären*), he tends to dismiss Paul's interpretation as a misconstrual. If an interpreter also includes the dimension of understanding (*verstehen*), he tends to defend Paul's interpretation as a true rendering of the text's true referent, even if different from the Old Testament's original sense.

Regardless of which of these hermeneutical stances one adopts, both exegetical moves are to be sharply distinguished from an approach which suggests that a modern Christian exegete can simply adopt Paul's method and read back into the Old Testament the full content of the Christian message when guided by the freedom of the Spirit (see Hays' sophisticated model of this alternative, 1989:154ff.). There are several historical and theological reasons against this form of allegory. First, it is historically unacceptable because it changes the voice of the original witness. Secondly, it is theologically unacceptable because it confuses a biblical word of promise with that of fulfillment by identifying the Old Testament with the New. Finally, it is hermeneutically in error by assuming that every time-conditioned feature of the New Testament can be used as a warrant for its continued use without properly understanding the theological relation of its authority to its function as kerygmatic witness. Of course this is the crucial distinction which separates genuine theological reflection on the Bible from every form of biblicism which imitates the biblical form without understanding its true content.

The Theological Task of Biblical Theology

With this hermeneutical sketch as a background, it is now time to focus specifically on the hermeneutical role of Biblical Theology. This discipline has as its fundamental goal to understand the various voices within the whole Christian Bible, New and Old Testament alike, as a witness to the one Lord Jesus Christ, the selfsame divine reality. The Old Testament bears testimony to the Christ who has not yet come; the New to the Christ who has appeared in the fullness of time. The two testaments do not relate to each other simply on the level of their role as witnesses. To remain on the textual level is to miss the key that unites dissident voices into a harmonious whole. Rather Biblical Theology attempts to hear the different voices in relation to the divine reality to which they point in such diverse ways. In one sense, this appeal is to a *Sachkritik* (a critique in terms of its content), but one in which the *Sache* is defined in such a way as to do justice to the witness of both testaments. An additional problem with adopting this term is that in the past it has often involved a form of critical reductionism that set witness against *res* in radical antagonism, as if word and spirit were natural enemies.

The dialogical move of biblical theological reflection that is being suggested is from the partial grasp of fragmentary reality found in both testaments to the full reality that the Christian church confesses to have found in Jesus Christ, in the combined witness of the two testaments. It is not the case that the New Testament writers possess a full knowledge of Christ which knowledge then corrects the Old Testament. Nor is it adequate to understand interpretation as moving only in the one direction of Old Testament to New. Rather both testaments bear testimony to the one Lord, in different ways, at different times, to different peoples, and yet both are understood and rightly heard in the light of the living Lord himself, the perfect reflection of the glory of God (Hebrews 1:3).

We have hitherto argued that biblical exegesis moves dialogically between text and reality. Biblical Theology has a similar movement, but extends the hermeneutical circle in several directions. Its critical focus lies in pursuing the different aspects of that reality testified to in multiple forms in the biblical texts of both testaments, and in seeking to establish a theological relationship. Proverbs 8 bears witness to wisdom, who was created by God at the beginning and who was with God at the creation of the world; John 1 testifies to a divine *logos* (word) with God at the beginning and through whom all things were made and who became flesh. It is a primary task of Biblical Theology to explore theologically the relation between this reality testified to in two different ways.

There is another essential part of the reflective enterprise of Biblical Theology that moves the discipline even more closely into the theological arena. Biblical Theology seeks not only to pursue the nature of the one divine reality among the various biblical voices, it also wrestles theologically with the relation between the reality testified to in the Bible and that living reality known and experienced as the exalted Christ through the Holy Spirit within the present community of faith. These two vehicles of revelation—Word and Spirit—are neither to be identified, nor are they to be separated and played one against the other.

The enterprise of Biblical Theology is theological because by faith seeking understanding in relation to the divine reality, the divine imperatives are no longer moored in the past, but continue to confront the hearer in the present as truth. Therefore it is constitutive of Biblical Theology that it be normative and not merely descriptive, and that it be responsive to the imperatives of the present and not just of the past.

There is yet another important hermeneutical dimension of Biblical Theology to be included. Because Biblical Theology grapples with the reality of the biblical witnesses, and moves beyond the original historical moorings of the text, the accusation is often made that such a model is anti-historical, philosophically idealistic, and abstract. Such a characterization badly misunderstands the approach that is being suggested. Biblical theological reflection is not timeless speculation about the nature of the good, but the life and death struggle of the concrete historical communities of the Christian church who are trying to be faithful in their own particular historical contexts to the imperatives of the gospel in mission to the world. But the heart of the enterprise is christological; its content is Jesus Christ and not its own self-understanding or identity. Therefore the aim of the enterprise involves the classic movement of faith seeking knowledge, of those who confess Christ struggling to understand the nature and will of the One who has already been revealed as Lord. The true expositor of the Christian scriptures is the one who awaits in anticipation toward becoming the interpreted rather than the interpreter. The very divine reality which the interpreter strives to grasp, is the very One who grasps the interpreter. The Christian doctrine of the role of the Holy Spirit is not a hermeneutical principle, but that divine reality itself who makes understanding of God possible.

There is one additional problem to be discussed in describing the nature of Biblical Theology. The emphasis up to now has been on the exegetical move from witness to reality, and then the specific biblical theological task of pursuing theologically the nature of this reality throughout the entire Christian canon. Now we raise a different sort of question. In what sense within Biblical Theology is there a movement in the reverse direction, namely, from the reality back to the biblical witness? Can interpreters—following their theological reflection toward a fuller grasp of a Christian understanding of the divine reality—now read this larger understanding back into the text? (See the discussion in Louth 1983.)

Initially it might seem that we have already flatly rejected this option as a form of illegitimate allegory. We have argued that the modern interpreter cannot simply imitate Paul's interpretation of the Old Testament and to do so is a form of biblicism. The reason behind this resistance is that such a move usually assumes that the original meaning of the Old Testament has lost its theological significance in the light of the New Testament, and that Paul's rendering of the Old Testament presents the one true sense of the text. Such a biblicist move not only undercuts the continuing canonical role of the Old Testament as Christian sculpture, but also avoids the required theological reflection which is an essential part of Christian theology.

Yet it also seems to me true that after the task of biblical theological reflection has begun in which the original integrity of both testaments has been respected, there is an important function of hearing the whole of Christian scripture in the light of the full reality of God in Jesus Christ. In other words, there is a legitimate place for a move from a fully developed Christian theological reflection back to the biblical texts of both testaments.

The reasons are far different from the biblicist attempt to recover the one true interpretation in which the Old Testament's hidden agenda was always Jesus Christ. It rather has to do with the ability of biblical language to resonate in a new and creative fashion when read from the vantage point of a fuller understanding of Christian truth. Such a reading is not intended to threaten the literal sense of the text (*sensus literalis*), but to extend through figuration a reality that has been only partially heard. It is for this reason that allegory or typology, when properly understood and practiced, remains an essential part of Christian interpretation and reflects a different understanding of how biblical reality is rendered than, say, midrash does within Judaism.

In the light of this dynamic understanding of the discipline of Biblical Theology the role of the history of interpretation—more properly named *Wirkungsgeschichte*—takes on its true significance within the enterprise (see Luz 1985). The history of interpretation serves as a continual reminder that biblical interpretation involves far more than "explanation" (*erklären*), but demands a serious wrestling with the content of scripture. The history of interpretation demonstrates clearly that when occasionally scholarship calls this into question, it rightly evokes a theological explosion from the side of the church (Kierkegaard, Kähler, Barth, etc.).

Then again, the history of interpretation serves as a major check against all forms of biblicism in showing the distance between the biblical text and the interpreter and the degree to which the changing situation of the reader affects one's hearing of the text. This observation should not lead to cultural relativism, but to a profounder grasp of the dynamic function of the Bible as the vehicle of an ever-fresh word of God to each new generation. It is a strange irony that those examples of biblical interpretation in the past that have truly immersed themselves in a specific concrete historical context, such as Luther in Saxony, retain the greatest value as models for the future actualization of the biblical text in a completely different world. Conversely those biblical commentators who laid claim to an objective, scientific explanation of what the text really meant, often appear as uninteresting museum pieces to the next generation.

Finally, the history of biblical interpretation often shows examples of the reading of scripture from the vantage point of a fully developed Christian theology that cannot be dismissed as fanciful allegory. Consider Milton on Genesis. Such examples illustrate in a profound way the ability of creative resonance of the text to illuminate the concrete life of Christian communities of faith through the study of scripture. Part of the task of modern Biblical Theology is to provide a proper context for understanding various usages of the Bible for shaping Christian identity that is of a very different order from modern historical critical exegesis.

The Relation between Biblical Theology and Dogmatics

One final topic to be discussed concerns the relation of this model of Biblical Theology to the discipline of dogmatic or systematic theology. Much has been written in recent years respecting this issue (see Rahner 1964; Schlier 1968; Hasel 1984; etc.). The problem is complex and controversial because the concept of dogmatic theology is presently just as much in flux as is Biblical Theology. It is also a question how much is gained through theoretical precision when the practical relationship is largely formed by the diverse training of these two groups of scholars. Modern biblical scholars generally know little about dogmatics, while conversely systematic theologians are woefully trained in the Bible (see the preface of Schillebeeckx 1979).

As is well known, the relationship between the two disciplines has gone through different stages. There was Biblical Theology's initial struggle for independence from dogmatics, followed by a period of mutual hostility and distrust, to a stage of separate and uncertain coexistence (see Hasel 1984:115). Clearly what is now required is fruitful cooperation, not only between these two fields, but among a whole variety of other disciplines which impinge on the study of the Bible, such as philosophical, literary, and historical scholarship.

Because of the initial training and interest of biblical scholars, the weight of their contribution will remain concentrated largely on describing and interpreting biblical texts. Conversely systematic theologians bring a variety of philosophical, theological, and analytical tools to bear which are usually informed by the history of theology and which are invaluable in relating the study of the Bible to the subject matter of the Christian life in the modern world. If there is some overlap in approach, this can only be welcomed as a benefit.

In sum, at this juncture probably little more precision in theory is required other than to urge biblical scholars to be more systematic, and systematic theologians to be more biblical, and to get on with the task. The ultimate test of the success of co-operation between the two fields lies in the degree to which the biblical text and its subject matter are illumined. Neither Biblical Theology nor dogmatic theology is an end in itself, but rather they remain useful tools by which to enable a fresh access to the living voice of God in sacred scripture.

5
Canonical Categories for Structuring a Biblical Theology

In a previous chapter the case was made for holding that the specific characteristic of the canonical shaping of the two testaments into one Christian Bible lay in the preservation of two distinct witnesses to a common subject matter who is Jesus Christ. The peculiar nature of the Christian canon derives from the joining of the Old Testament witness in its own integrity with the New Testament witness in its own integrity. However, the witness of the latter is made to a large extent by means of an analogical use of the Old Testament.

The specific concern of this chapter is to reflect on the implications of this form of canonical shaping for the structuring of a Biblical Theology. One of the major criticisms of the traditional approaches to the subject—*dicta probantia, Heilsgeschichte*, traditio-historical—lies in their failure to take seriously those peculiar canonical features of the Christian Bible. What then are the implications of canon for the actual organizing of the enterprise?

First, it seems to me compatible to the canonical structure to describe the Old Testament's witness to God's redemptive will in the context of the history of Israel. It is an obvious, but essential feature of the Old Testament that the original addressee and tradent of this biblical witness was Israel, which sets this testament clearly apart from the New Testament. By means of a great variety of different literary genres the biblical witness of the Old Testament was made in constant relation to the history of this people. The once-for-all quality of historical events within a chronological sequence is a fundamental characteristic of the entire Old Testament witness. The Old Testament canon is structured in relation to a history of this people that sets it apart immediately from a theological tractate or philosophical dialogue. The Old Testament's understanding of God was set forth in a series of revelatory events which entered Israel's time and space. The Old Testament bears witness to the beginning of creation, the call of Abraham, the exodus from Egypt, the revelation at Sinai, the possession of the land, the establishment of the monarchy, the destruction of Jerusalem, exile and restoration.

Yet there are other features of the Old Testament that make clear that its witness is not that simply of a history book. Rather, the peculiar features of God's revelation in Israel's history has resulted in a far more complicated and intensified form of biblical response. The form of historical construal deviates greatly from the recording of sequential events. Seldom are the biblical events registered according to an absolute chronology, but the quality of the happenings usually takes precedence. There is a beginning and an ending of human history that is set within God's divine purpose. Israel's life is also recorded in terms of institutions, rulers, and a cultic calendar.

Another central characteristic of the Old Testament is that its witness to God's history of encounter with Israel was preserved in living traditions that were constantly being shaped by generations of tradents. In a variety of different ways the foundational, once-for-all events of Israel's history continued to be heard and reinterpreted as an ongoing witness to Israel's life with God. Thus, for example, the witness to God's initial act of creation in the book of Genesis was extended by the later prophets to include the hope of a new creation that would finally realize the divine plan. Conversely, other events such as the conquest of the land were not given an eschatological extension but rendered as an unrepeatable occurrence of the past. The kingship of Saul was interpreted theologically as a negative example of human failure, whereas the reign of David was rendered typologically as a form of the rule of God, or eschatologically as a foreshadowing of the Messiah, or sapientially as an enduring model of royal wisdom.

It would seem to be a fundamental task of

Biblical Theology that is done in accord with the canonical structuring carefully to describe the theological functions of the great revelatory events in Israel's history and their subsequent appropriation by the tradition. This enterprise would share, for example, with von Rad the conviction that a fruitful avenue into Old Testament theology is in terms of Israel's continual reflection on the great redemptive events of her history. Yet it would differ from von Rad in hearing the voice of Israel, not in the form of scientifically reconstructed streams of tradition, but in the canonically shaped literature of the Old Testament as the vehicle of Israel's *Heilsgeschichte.* Both approaches have in common hearing the peculiar form of the Old Testament witness through the form that the historical tridents of the tradition gave the material rather than seeing the uninterpreted historical events themselves as the avenues to an understanding of God's intent.

Secondly, it seems to me compatible to the canonical structure to describe the New Testament's witness to God's redemption through Jesus Christ in the context of the early church. The Evangelists bear witness to the life, death, and resurrection of Jesus Christ as God's salvation of the world, and the Apostles further testify to the effect of this gospel on the formation of the church. The New Testament proclaims the new story of Jesus Christ. Its witness is not merely an extension of the Old Testament nor is it a redactional layer to Israel's history. The direction from which the New Testament's testimony arose was from the revolutionary encounter with the risen Lord. The disciples had a new message to proclaim, a gospel, which was grounded in the historical concreteness of Jesus Christ, whose life unfolded at a particular time in Palestine, under Roman rule, from Jewish parents.

There are striking discontinuities between the New and the Old Testaments that confirm the canonical ordering of the two distinct collections of sacred writings. The Greek language and Hellenistic culture stand in contrast to the Hebrew-Aramaic Old Testament. The tradent of the New Testament is the Christian church, not the Jewish synagogue, which increasingly emerges in an antagonistic or at least a critical relation to traditional Jewish religious institutions. The New Testament is directed primarily to the nations, and only indirectly to Israel, in the light of the Jewish rejection of Jesus. Finally, the Christian experience of the gospel as a radically new revelation of God sets its sacred writings consciously in opposition to Moses, as the representative of the old.

Nevertheless, the most striking feature of the New Testament is that it bears its witness to the radically new in terms of the old. The gospel of Jesus Christ is understood by means of a transformed Old Testament. The writers of the New Testament began from their experience with

Jesus Christ from whom they received a radically new understanding of the Jewish scriptures. Then on the basis of this transformed Old Testament, the New Testament writers interpreted the theological significance of Jesus Christ to the Christian church by means of the Old. Moreover, the historical uniqueness of Jesus of Nazareth was not only related theologically to Israel's traditions of the past, but extended into the future by means of eschatological and liturgical actualization.

It would seem to me to be a major enterprise of Biblical Theology to describe carefully both the continuity and discontinuity between these two different witnesses of the Christian Bible. It will be important to see to what extent a trajectory of Old Testament traditions, such as the exodus, has been picked up and continued within the New Testament, or has been reshaped, transformed, and even broken off. There is an equal need to investigate those cases in which the New Testament made no use of the Old Testament, but stood at a great distance from its tradition history. There will be times in which the New Testament's use of the Old Testament is highly selective, or one in which a single component is employed as a critical norm against other major streams of tradition. Only after this descriptive task has been done will it be possible to turn to the larger task of trying to engage in theological reflection of the whole Christian Bible in the light of its subject matter of which it is a witness.

Abbreviations

BET	Beiträge zur evangelischen Theologie
BTZ	*Berliner Theologische Zeitschrift*
ET	English translation
EvTh	*Evangelische Theologie*
GPT	Growing Points in Theology
HSM	Harvard Semitic Monographs
HTS	Harvard Theological Studies
IDB	*Interpreter's Dictionary of the Bible*
IDBSup	*IDB Supplmentary Volume*
JAAR	*Journal of the American Academy of Religion*
JBR	*Journal of Bible and Religion*
JBTh	*Jahrbuch für biblische Theologie*
JSOTSup	Journal for the Study of the Old Testament Supplement Series
KJV	King James Version (Authorized Version)
LXX	Septuagint
MTS	Marburger Theologische Studien
OTL	Old Testament Library
PTMS	Princeton Theological Monograph Series
RE	*Realencyklopädie für protestantische Theologie und Kirche*
RGG²	*Die Religion in Geschichte und Gegenwart,* 2nd ed. (1927–31)
SBT	Studies in Biblical Theology
SJT	*Scottish Journal of Theology*
TJ	*Trinity Journal*
TLZ	*Theologische Literaturzeitung*
TRE	*Theologische Realenzyklopädie*
TZ	*Theologische Zeitschrift*
ZNW	*Zeitschrift für die neutestamentliche Wissenschaft und die Kunde der älteren Kirche*
ZTK	*Zeitschrift für Theologie und Kirche*

Bibliography

Aland, Kurt, editor. 1968. *The Greek New Testament.* 2nd ed. New York: United Bible Societies.

Ammon, C. F. 1792. *Antwurf einer reinen biblischen Theologie.* Erlangen: n.p.

Barr, James. 1976. "Biblical Theology." In *IDBSup*, 104–11.

Barr, James. 1983. *Holy Scripture: Canon, Authority, Criticism.* Philadelphia: Westminster.

Bauer, Georg Lorenz. 1796. *Theologie des Alten Testaments.* 2 vols. Leipzig: Weyand.

———. 1800–1802. *Biblische Theologie des Neuen Testaments.* Vols. 1–4. Leipzig: Weyand.

Beckwith, Roger. 1985. *The Old Testament Canon of the New Testament Church.* Grand Rapids: Eerdmans.

Breukelman, F. H. 1980. *Bijbelse Theologie.* Vol. 1/1. Kampen: Kok.

Brueggemann, Walter. 1991. "Canonization and Contextualization." In *Interpretation and Obedience: From Faithful Reading to Faithful Living*, 119–42. Philadelphia: Fortress Press.

Buhl, Frants Peter William. 1892. *Canon and Text of the Old Testament.* Translated by J. MacPherson. Edinburgh: T. & T. Clark.

Bultmann, Rudolf. 1951–55. *Theology of the New Testament.* 2 vols. Translated by K. Grobel. New York: Scribner.

Childs, Brevard S. 1970. *Biblical Theology in Crisis.* Philadelphia: Westminster.

———. 1979. *Introduction to the Old Testament as Scripture.* Philadelphia: Fortress Press.

———. 1985. *The New Testament as Canon: An Introduction.* Philadelphia: Fortress Press.

———. 1992. "Die Bedeutung der hebräischen Bibel für die biblische Theologie." *TZ* 48:382–99.

———. 1993. *Biblical Theology of the Old and New Testaments: Theological Reflections on the Christian Bible.* Minneapolis: Fortress Press.

Clements, R. E. 1975. *Prophecy and Tradition.* GPT. Atlanta: John Knox.

Coggins, R. J. 1975. *Samaritans and Jews: The Origins of Samaritanism Reconsidered.* GPT. Atlanta: John Knox.

Cross, Frank Moore Jr. 1975. "The Evolution of a Theory of Local Texts." In *Qumran and the History of Biblical Text,* edited by F. M. Cross and S. Talmon, 306–20. Cambridge: Harvard Univ. Press.

Diestel, Ludwig. 1869. *Geschichte des Alten Testamentes in der christlichen Kirche.* Jena: Mauke.

Dulles, Avery. 1965. "Response to Krister Stendahl's 'Method in Biblical Theology.'" In *The Bible in Modern Scholarship,* edited by J. P. Hyatt, 210–16. Nashville: Abingdon.

Ebeling, Gerhard. 1963. "The Meaning of 'Biblical Theology.'" In *Word and Faith,* 79–97. Translated by J. W. Leitch. Philadelphia: Fortress Press.

———. 1971. *Lutherstudien.* Vol. 1. Tübingen: Mohr/Siebeck.

Eissfeldt, Otto. 1965. *The Old Testament: An Introduction.* Translated by P. R. Ackroyd. New York: Harper & Row.

Ewald, Heinrich. 1871–76. *Die Lehre der Bibel von*

Gott; oder, Theologie des Alten und Neuen Bundes. Vols. 1–4. Leipzig: Vogel.

Filson, Floyd V. 1957. *Which Books Belong in the Bible? A Study of the Canon*. Philadelphia: Westminster.

Flacius, Matthias (Illyricus). 1580. *Clavis scripturae sacrae*, Basel: n.p.

Frei, Hans. 1973. *The Eclipse of Biblical Narrative: A Study in Eighteenth and Nineteenth Century Hermeneutics*. New Haven: Yale Univ. Press.

Gabler, Johann Philipp. 1787. "De justo discrimine theologiae biblique et dogmaticae regundisque recte utrius que finibus." Translated as "J. P. Gabler and the Distinction between Biblical and Dogmatic Theology." *SJT* 33 (1980) 133–58.

Gese, Hartmut. 1970. "Erwägungen zur Einheit der biblischen Theologie." *ZTK* 67:417–36. Reprinted in *Vom Sinai zum Zion: Alttestamentliche Beitrage zur biblische Theologie*, 11–30. BET 64. Munich: Kaiser, 1974.

Gunkel, Hermann. 1927. "Biblische Theologie und biblische Religionsgeschichte: I. des AT." In *RGG²* 1:1089–91.

Gunneweg, A. H. J. 1978. *Understanding the Old Testament*. Translated by J. Bowden. OTL. Philadelphia: Westminster.

Hasel, Gerhard F. 1984. "The Relationship between Biblical Theology and Systematic Theology." *TJ* 5:113–27.

Hays, Richard B. 1989. *Echoes of Scripture in the Letters of Paul*. New Haven: Yale Univ. Press.

Holtzmann, Heinrich Julius. 1911. *Lehrbuch der neutestamentlichen Theologie*. Vol. 1. 2nd ed. Tubingen: Mohr.

Hornig, Gottfried. 1961. *Die Anfänge der historisch-kritischen Theologie: Johann Salomo Semlers*

Schriftverstandnis und seine Stellung zu Luther.
Forschungen zur systematischen Theologie und
Religionsphilosophie 8. Göttingen: Vanden-
hoeck & Ruprecht.

Hübner, Hans. 1990. *Biblische Theologie des Neuen
Testaments.* Vol. 1. Göttingen: Vandenhoeck &
Ruprecht.

Janowski, Bernd. 1986. "Literatur zur Biblischen
Theologie 1982–85." *JBTh* 1:210–44.

Jepsen, Alfred. 1949. "Kanon und Text des Alten
Testaments." *TLZ* 74:66–74.

Jugie, Martin. 1904. *Histoire du canon de l'Ancien
Testament dan l'église grecque et l'église russe.*
Études de théologie orientale 1. Paris: Beauch-
esne.

Kähler, Martin. 1896. "Biblische Theologie." In *RE³*
3:192–200.

Katz, P. 1956. "The Old Testament Canon in Palestine
and Alexandria." *ZNW* 47:191–217.

Kelsey, David H. 1980. "The Bible and Christian Theology." *JAAR* 48:385–402.

Kraus, Hans-Joachim. 1970. *Die biblische Theologie:
Ihre Geschichte und Problematik.* Neukirchen-
Vluyen: Neukirchener.

Leiman, Sid Z. 1976. *The Canonization of Hebrew
Scripture: The Talmudic and Midrashic Evidence.* Hamden, Conn.: Archon. (2nd ed. 1991.)

Lewis, J. P. 1964. "What do we mean by Jabneh?"
JBR 32:125–32.

Louth, A. 1983. *Discerning the Mystery: An Essay on
the Nature of Theology.* Oxford: Clarendon.

Luz, Ulrich. 1985. "Wirkungsgeschichtliche Exegese."
BTZ 2:18–32.

Margolis, Max L. 1922. *The Hebrew Scriptures in the
Making.* Philadelphia: Jewish Publication Society of America.

Merk, Otto. 1972. *Biblische Theologie des Neuen Tes-tamentes in ihrer Anfangszeit: Ihre methodis-chen Probleme bei Johann Philipp Gabler und Georg Lorenz Bauer und deren Nachwirkungen.* MTS 9. Marburg: Elwert.

————. 1980. "Biblische Theologie II. Neues Testa-ment." In *TRE* 6:455–77.

Metzger, Bruce M. 1987. *The Canon of the New Tes-tament: Its Origin, Development, and Signifi-cance.* Oxford: Clarendon.

Moore, George F. 1911. "The Definition of the Jewish Canon and the Repudiation of Christian Scrip-tures." In *C. A. Briggs Testimonial: Essays in Modern Theology,* New York, 99–125. Reprinted in *Canon and Masorah of the Hebrew Bible,* edited by S. Z. Leiman, 115–41.

Morgan, Robert, editor and translator. 1973. *The Nature of New Testament Theology: The contri-bution of William Wrede and Adolf Schlatter.* SBT 2/25. Naperville, Ill.: Allenson.

Oehler, Gustav F. 1883. *Theology of the Old Testa-ment.* Translated by G. E. Day. Rev. ed. New York: Funk & Wagnalls.

Oeming, Manfred. 1987. *Gesamtbiblische Theologien der Gegenwart: Das Verhältnis von AT und NT in der hermeneutischen Diskussion seit Gerhard von Rad.* 2nd ed. Stuttgart: Kohlhammer.

Ollenburger, Ben C. 1985. "Biblical Theology: Situat-ing the Discipline." In *Understanding the Word: Essays in Honour of Bernhard W. Anderson,* edited by J. T. Butler and B. C. Ollenburger, 37–62. JSOTSup 37. Sheffield: JSOT Press.

Preuss, Horst Dietrich. 1984. *Das Alte Testament in christlicher Predigt.* Stuttgart: Kohlhammer.

Purvis, J. D. 1968. *The Samaritan Pentateuch and the Origin of the Samaritan Sect.* HSM 2. Cambridge: Harvard Univ. Press.

Rad, Gerhard von. 1965. *Old Testament Theology.* Vol. 2: *The Theology of Israel's Prophetic Traditions.* Translated by D. M. G. Stalker. New York: Harper & Row.

Rahner, Karl. 1964. "Exegesis and Dogmatic Theology." In *Dogmatic vs Biblical Theology,* ed. H. Vorgrimler, 31–65. Baltimore: Helicon.

Reuss, Edward. 1891. *History of the Canon of the Holy Scripture in the Christian Church.* Translated by D. Hunter. 2nd ed. Edinburgh: Hunter.

Reventlow, Henning Graf von. 1986. *Problems of Biblical Theology in the Twentieth Century.* Translated by J. Bowden. Philadelphia: Fortress Press.

Rüger, Hans Peter. 1988. "Das Werden des christlichen Alten Testaments." *JBTh* 3:175–89.

Ryle, Herbert Edward. 1892. *The Canon of the Old Testament: An Essay on the Gradual Growth and Formation of the Hebrew Canon of Scripture.* New York: Macmillan.

Schillebeeckx, Edward. 1979. *Jesus: An Experiment in Christology.* Translated by H. Hoskins. New York: Crossroad.

Schlier, Heinrich. 1968. "Biblical and Dogmatic Theology." In *The Relevance of the New Testament,* 26–38. Translated by W. J. O'Hara. New York: Herder and Herder.

Schultz, Hermann. 1898. *Old Testament Theology.* 2 vols. Translated by J. A. Paterson. 2nd ed. Edinburgh: T. & T. Clark.

Smend, Rudolf. 1957. *Wilhelm Martin Leberecht de Wettes Arbeit am Alten und Neuen Testament.* Basel: Helbing & Lichtenhahn.

———. 1962. "Johann Philipp Gablers Begründung der biblischen Theologie." *EvTh* 22:345–57.

Stendahl, Krister. 1962. "Biblical Theology, Contemporary." In *IDB* 1:418–32.

———. 1965. "Method in Biblical Theology." In *The Bible in Modern Scholarship*, edited by J. P. Hyatt, 196–209. Nashville: Abingdon.

Stuhlmacher, Peter. 1979. *Vom Verstehen des Neuen Testaments: Eine Hermeneutik*. Göttingen: Vandenhoeck & Ruprecht. (2nd ed. 1986.)

———. 1986. *Reconciliation, Law and Righteousness: Essays in Biblical Theology*. Translated by E. R. Kalin. Philadelphia: Fortress Press.

Sundberg, Albert C. 1964. *The Old Testament of the Early Church*. HTS 22. Cambridge: Harvard Univ. Press.

Swanson, Theodore N. 1970. "The Closing of the Collection of Holy Scripture: A Study in the History of the Canonization of the Old Testament." Ph.D. diss. Vanderbilt University.

Tillich, Paul. 1957. *Systematic Theology*. Vol. 2. Chicago: Univ. of Chicago Press.

Torrance, Alan. 1989. "Does God Suffer? Incarnation and Impassibility." In *Christ in Our Place: The Humanity of God in Christ for the Reconciliation of the World. Essays Presented to Professor James Torrance*, edited by T. A. Hart and D. P. Thimell, 315–68. PTMS 25. Allison Park, Pa.: Pickwick.

Tracy, David. 1981. *The Analogical Imagination: Christian Theology and the Culture of Pluralism*. New York: Crossroad.

Wildeboer, G. 1895. *The Origin of the Canon of the Old Testament: A Historico-Critical Inquiry*. Translated by B. W. Bacon. London: Luzac.

Vatke, Wilhelm. 1835. *Die Religion des Alten Testamentes*. Vol. 1. Berlin: Bethge.

de Wette, W. M. L. 1813. *Biblische Dogmatik Alten*

und Neuen Testaments. Berlin.

Zachariä, Gotthilf Traugott. 1771–72. *Biblische Theologie.* Vols. 1–4. Göttingen: Bossiegel.

Zahn, Theodor. 1888. *Geschichte des neutestamentlichen Kanon.* Vol. 1. Erlangen: Deichert.

Zimmerli, Walther. 1980. "Biblische Theologie I.
Altes Testament." In *TRE* 6:426–55.